THE EYE OF A NEEDLE

"For it is easier for a camel to go through a needle's eye, than for a rich man to enter into the kingdom of God."

- Luk 18:25

1. INTRODUCTION

I quoted the above from the Bible, that it is easier for a Camel to go through a needle's eye, than for a rich man to enter into the Kingdom of God. The same is also written in Mat 19:24 and Mar 10:25.

I understand from the above that riches corrupt a person's soul, and it cuts off the line of communication that exists with the Lord.

In this book, I am going to investigate this whole scenario of just how it is that riches can corrupt a person, and how we are all potential victims, but I am also going to provide you with answers to the problem, with solutions to one of the biggest enemies of our time....money.

Too many books have been written where there are so many quotations from the Bible that it appears as if some tried to rewrite the Bible, which is the main reason why I am going to keep quotes from the Bible to a bare minimum.

I am writing all chapters in layman's terms, in a way that it will be easy to read and even easier to relate to. Only in the second last Chapter, I found it necessary to copy more versus from the Bible, to lend authority to the points I am putting across.

2. MONEY MAKES THE WORLD GO ROUND

Money makes the world go round, a saying dating back to the 1930's, meant to be a humoristic comment on the worlds need for money. How sad isn't it that the saying isn't far from wrong…

We need money in our everyday lives, to buy food like our daily bread, sugar, coffee, tea, and so on. Without money, in these modern days, people do not grow their own crops anymore, don't keep their own cattle, and are therefore completely dependant on the "system", which is run and controlled by money.

We need to pay for the electricity or gas we use, paying off that mortgage on a house, paying for fuel, and we need money to go to the convenient store.

Those who don't have money will eventually starve to death, while others earn just enough money to get by.

There are organizations like UNICEF that tries their best to help feed starving nations, but even with the contributions these organizations make, not all people can be saved. In our daily lives, we see homeless people walking the streets, begging for food, just food, because they are hungry.

Yes, it is true that some of them drink alcohol in all forms and shapes, but the reason for that is simple, if you consume alcohol, you don't get hungry as often and when you do eat, you don't have a huge appetite.

It is also better for some to lay somewhere drunk, and not know that you are hungry, than it is to be sober and very conscious of your aching tummy and your need for food, any food.

In this day and age, more and more people work, just so that they can afford a small place to live in, and so that they can buy food, and only the bare essentials. There is no money left for anything else.

Money is a scarce commodity, and people over the world are very much aware of that. Everybody has a need "just to have enough money" to get by on, and they really mean it, but what is "just enough" money?

3. FROM NEED TO GREED

Money is needed to pay for food and other important things, and to have the need for money in that context is justified, but when the need for money exceeds what is necessary, it becomes greed, and greed for money can change a person for the worse.

When greed takes over a person's life, that person looses touch with reality and *become immune towards other peoples feelings*, because the Holy Spirit is no more part of that person.

I know it sounds terrible, but when you choose to be greedy, you literally chase away the Holy Spirit for the sake of following mammon.

Greed alone is all that is needed to prevent a person from going to heaven, that is why the Lord warns us against trying to make money in haste (Pro 28:22).

It is so easy for a person to be overcome by greed, since there are no warning sign to look out for, no way how we can tell that money is busy corrupting our soul by taking over our lives.

Greed may wrongfully be misinterpreted by some as need, but while need comprises only the necessary, greed goes beyond that, craving more than what is necessary, and still more. *Greed is insatiable.*

4. THE GLORIFICATION OF MONEY

Money is glorified on TV shows, the National Lotto, advertisements, Casino's. Everywhere you look you will see neon money signs inviting you to be the next millionaire, or you can win a million underneath a cool drink bottle cap.

The idea is floating around that anybody can become rich overnight, and this has the effect that people literally spend money *which they don't have* in casinos, on the lotto, and in other places, for the hope of making a quick fortune.

Maybe, just maybe they can walk away rich, but what they are not thinking about, and what no one will ever tell them, is that the stakes are so high because the chances that anyone will win all that money are slimmer than slim, almost impossible.

The system is designed to trick people out of their money, *forcing them to slave for Mammon.*

Look at what type of people are regular visitors at casinos, old people and others who cannot afford to buy themselves a decent meal, people who are easily lured into the trap.

These people will loose their entire salary on gambling, sometimes even in one day, but they will return again and again to try and make up for the money that they lost, and they all hope (and maybe even pray!!) to win the jackpot one day…, but they never do.

These people all became greedy, and that is why they will keep on going back, and keep on spending the little money they have to feed the machines and poker tables. *They truly have become slaves of the system, and can't turn back.*

Who do you think is the mastermind of the system?, it is none other than satan himself.

People visit loan sharks to borrow money so that they can buy what they never could afford in the first place, overcome by greed and not thinking about having to pay back the loan and the interest on that loan.

When it finally becomes time to pay back the loan, they find that they are in a predicament, and take out another loan somewhere else to cover the first one, and so it goes on, and each time the strap gets pulled tighter, causing suffering and misery that could have been avoided.

I just created these two scenarios so that you can see how greed can destroy lives. Now, let us look at those people who "*make it*" in the *world*, who manages to *accumulate* wealth on earth.

These people may have suffered at some stage, but they have been alleviated to the point where they never have to suffer anymore. *To these people, money means everything.*

They can buy what they want and go where they want, but like I said before, because they are greedy, they always want more and are never content, with what they have.

When you are rich, your value system would almost certainly change. Because you can more or less buy anything, you tend to lose respect for the things that count in life.

One way where it would be very obvious in is the way in which you treat others, almost like they are your pheasants.

5. LOOSING TOUCH WITH REALITY

Rich people easily loose touch with reality, because they tend to live in their own little world of comfort which they created for themselves, *where they are the masters and above everyone else.*

Because all their basic needs are catered for automatically, they loose their appreciation for it, and take it for granted. They have *accumulated* so much that they never have to worry about how they will put the next plate of food on the table.

They start to see themselves not only as better off than others, but as *better*, period. The exotic sort of lifestyle they lead also contributes to them alienating themselves from the ordinary man on the street.

There only concern is to maintain the lifestyles they lead, and it always involves money and more money. Those extravagant lifestyles cost a lot to maintain.

Because these rich people have what they want and more, they forget how to ask God for things, and become totally self reliant. *They care more about their riches than anything else.* They spend time with their stockbrokers, not on a God that doesn't answer them back.

They are earth bound, and would do anything to protect their earthly possessions. They lose trust in God, *and only trust in their riches.*

God says that they who trust in their riches shall fall, and they who are righteous, shall flourish as a branch.

The Bible speaks of rich people who become high-minded, which means arrogant.

To increase their riches, rich people may even start to *oppress the poor people, and become wicked.*

6. THE MIND OF A RICH MAN

To the rich man, the laws of the common people don't apply. Rich people feel exalted above the normal, hardworking person.

In their minds, they need to be treated differently, and with a great deal of respect, just because they are rich. They are cut off from the reality of life by the same thing that brings them "happiness", and that is their money.

Not all rich people are the same, but in most cases, they develop a character that they think would best suit their status, and start to live like that character.

They forget who they were and where they came from, and only concentrate on their new character and their money.

They are very skeptic about other people and their motives, and lost the ability to trust others.

Their minds have gotten accustomed to thinking about the physical and not the spiritual. Their minds focus on what the world has to offer, and gets drawn deeper and deeper in all the earthly pleasures which they can afford.

They use the money of this world to accumulate things from this world, so their whole mindset has changed to be of this world.

The rich not only don't see the necessity to pray, but they also don't worship the Lord anymore. In their minds, they have everything that money can buy, and they don't owe anybody anything, including God.

7. GIVING AND SHARING

The richer you become, the less you'll feel like giving to others. You will feel that you worked hard for your money and won't just give money away, it is your money.

You will start to think that other people are undeserving, and that you are entitled to keep your money to yourself.

Rich people will only share with those who they carefully selected, and don't care about anybody else who might be suffering, who are in need.

To give without receiving isn't practiced by rich people. They always demand a return on their investment.

I have seen once on Television a man worth Billions of Dollars, about 260 Billion in total, earning about 30 Million a day with all his businesses, donating one Million Dollars towards charity. Why would this man donate only one million when he could give away millions and millions to enrich the lives of so many more people? Truth is, he only did that to draw attention to himself, an investment so that people may take notice of him.

Look at all the so called superstars in Hollywood. They have more money than they can spend in a lifetime. Some of them get involved with organizations to help the poor, but they only contribute enough to market themselves.

You will never see any of these people making a true commitment, which is because they still want to remain rich, so that they don't fall in to the same category as the people they "represent".

As long as they can be perceived as idols and superstars, they are ok with it, but don't ask them to donate more than they are.

They see the opportunity to help those in need as a cheap way of marketing themselves to become even more rich and famous.

8. THEIR WILL, NOT GODS WILL

The rich has long forgotten to follow God and do His will. All they know is their will. Since they don't have to ask God for anything, why should they still do what God wants them to do? They follow their own will in what they do from day to day, without hesitation or the desire to change.

Where God wants them to be righteous, they are self-righteous; believing that what they do is right, regardless of what they do. They will justify all they do in the act of that belief.

They see nothing wrong in the enjoyment of life. They travel to exotic destinations and meet people from all over the world, buy expensive cars and houses, so why should they give it up when they worked hard for their money?

They are stubborn to the point of listening only to themselves, and will not give that up easily.

Rich people are in fact also tempting God's mercy because the think they can buy anything with their money, even good health. It is also common for the rich to see Tarot readers on a regular basis, where they spend thousands just to get a good reading.

They either forgot that tarot readings are from the occult (satan), or they simply don't care.

It is any rich mans fantasy to live forever, so they will spend fortunes on remedies and treatments in order to stay young, to cheat death, so that they can enjoy their riches for longer.

In order for the rich to follow God, they have to change their extravagant way of living, and that alone is more than most can bear.

Rich people are also identified by their *vanity*. They regard themselves as very important, and expect others also to treat them as such.

They are arrogant in their ways and expect to be treated with the utmost of respect, just short of bowing down to. In some cases, the rich literally forces their staff to bow down before them, as if they are gods!!

10. WHAT DOES THE BIBLE SAY?

In order to give a better illustration in this Chapter, I will be quoting a couple of versus from the Bible.

James 5 verses 1 through 6 read as follow: "*Come now, ye rich men, weep and howl for your miseries that shall come upon you. Your riches are corrupted and your garments are moth-eaten, your gold and silver are rusted and the rust of them shall be a witness against you and shall eat your flesh as it were fire. You have hoarded treasure together for the last days. Behold the hire of the laborers who have reaped down your fields which is of you kept back by fraud cries out and the cries of them who have reaped are entered into the years of the Lord of sabaoth. Ye have lived in pleasure on the earth and been wanton; ye have nourished your hearts as in a day of slaughter; ye have condemned and killed the just and he does not resist you."*

Most of the truth that you see in this passage seems to be being lived out before our very eyes. In fact, not just before our eyes but the whole world has seen the love of riches and what it produces of wickedness on a far-reaching scale.

We have been exposed to the opulence, the indulgence, the materialism, the myriad of houses and cars and boats and furs and jewelry and secret bank accounts and fraud and sexual sins and everything that goes with the materialistic way of living.

The ugliness of what we have seen needs explanation and the best way to understand it is from the Word of God. And so as we look at these verses you'll see them illustrated vividly in the scenario going on at this very time.

Now keep in mind that it is typical of James to be offering tests of living faith. All the way through this letter as he writes to a group of Christians in a local assembly, Jewish Christians, he calls them to evaluate the validity of their faith knowing that always where there is wheat, the devil over sows' tares, where there is the true there will be the false. And wanting to be sure that no one is under any illusion about being a Christian when in fact they're not.

And so all the way through the letter you have one test after another. And this is no different.

How a person feels about and handles wealth is a test. How you feel about money and possessions and material things is a test which reveals the spiritual state of your heart. James is obviously speaking to people who though on the outside they may affirm faith in Christ and love for God, obviously love money. And their life is totally controlled and governed by that love of money. And so their spiritual state is revealed in the matter of their relationship to riches.

James did not develop this test. James is merely repeating the test that our Lord began.

This is what our Lord said in Matthew 6:19 to 21, a very familiar passage. "*Lay not up for yourselves treasures upon earth where moth and rust corrupts and where thieves break through and steal, but lay up for yourselves treasures in heaven where neither moth nor rust corrupt and where thieves do not break through nor steal, for where your treasure is, there will your heart be also.*" This is a test.

You want to tell me where your heart is, show me where your treasure is. Where are you stockpiling your treasure? Where are you placing your wealth? That's the test that Jesus gave in the Sermon on the Mount.

In Luke 16:11, we find another example of where our Lord essentially did the same thing: "*If therefore you have not been faithful in the unrighteous money, who will commit to your trust the true riches?*"

To put the above in plain English…: "Do you think God will commit to you the realities of His eternal Kingdom which are the true riches if you have not demonstrated a proper handling of money?"

Will God give you what is really valuable if you can't handle what is not? If you have not been faithful in that which is another man's, who shall give you that which is your own? If you can't be faithful in the money that you manage as a stewardship from God, as it were, then why would God give you something of your own to possess with a spiritual nature?

And then He sums it up in Mat 6:24, "*No man can serve two masters, either he will hate the one and love the other or else he will hold to the one and despise the other, you cannot serve God and mammon.*" Off course, mammon in this context means wealth, money.

And the very next verse, Mat 6:25, "*And the Pharisees also who were covetous heard all these things and they derided Him.*" They were religious but the state of their heart was revealed in their covetousness.

It is a test, how you feel about wealth is a spiritual test.

Back to James chapter 5, James is really reiterating a test that our Lord Himself established. And the passage in James is a strong passage, the strongest in the epistle. It's a passage of damning judgment against the wicked wealthy who profess Christian faith and profess Christian life but whose real God is money.

James then is building on the teaching of the Lord Jesus as he often does. In fact there are really many parallels in the epistle of James to the Sermon on the Mount. And we see a direct parallel here with chapter 6 verses 19 and 21.

So he is calling on the wealthy to check the true state of their heart by how they're dealing with their wealth. And in this section he gives the most blistering, the most condemning, and the most scornful condemnation given in his epistle. It is against those wicked wealthy people who have been given the benefit of wealth but have perverted and corrupted it and themselves in the manner they have handled it.

They have prostituted the goodness of God who basically gives us the power to get wealth, as it says in Deuteronomy 8:18. They have prostituted the goodness and generosity and blessing of God of whom it says the blessing of the Lord brings wealth in Proverbs 10:22. They have taken what God generously and graciously has given and corrupted and perverted it.

Now let me say to you that wealth in itself is not sinful. I think you know that. It's not sinful to possess money. It's not sinful to possess the blessings that God would grant.

It is a stewardship given by God to some. All of us have some wealth to manage and it varies from person to person by God's design. And God can bless us in different ways, giving some of us more and some of us less than others.

It's not wrong to possess money, but obviously it's wrong to misuse it. By the way, the more you have the greater in many ways is the potential for prostituting its proper use. When, however, your heart is perverted and the love of money controls you, then it leads, according to 1 Timothy 6:10, to all kinds of evil. And it even leads to judgment, judgment by God Himself.

James is speaking then against the love of money that causes people to take that which is a blessing from God, pervert it for their own ends. They may say they're

Christians. They may belong to the church. They may go to the church. But James is saying you better take a look at what they do with their money because as Jesus taught, it will reveal the state of their heart. If they serve money, they don't serve God. If they're laying up all their treasure in earth, that's where their heart is. It's that simple.

We need to go back to the Old Testament to understand passage better. I want to quote some passages, so you'll understand what James is really saying. And it's a very rich kind of heritage that James places himself in as he speaks, as it were, like an Old Testament prophet. Read, for example, Isaiah chapter 3 verse 14. where Isaiah says, "*The Lord will enter into judgment with the ancients of His people and their princes for you have eaten up the vineyard, the spoil of the poor is in your houses. What mean you that you beat My people to pieces and grind the faces of the poor, says the Lord God of hosts.*" You have abused the poor, He is saying, for your own purposes and your own ends and you've consumed everything in sight.

Isaiah chapter 10, "*Woe unto them who decree unrighteous decrees, who have grievances which they have prescribed to turn aside the needy from justice, take away the right from the poor of my people, that widows may be their prey and that they may rob the fatherless. And what will you do in the day of visitation and in the desolation which shall come from far? To whom will you flee for help? And where will you leave your glory? Without Me they shall bow down unto the prisoners and they shall fall unto the slain for all this His anger is not turned away but His hand is stretched out still.*" Another strong denunciation of the ungodly for the way they have treated the poor and how they misused God's gift of wealth.

Nobody says it more directly than Amos. Amos the herdsman of Tekoa, chapter 4, "*Hear this word, you cows of Bashan, you fat cows, as it were, you've fattened yourselves up that are in the mountains of Samaria, who oppress the poor, who crush the needy, who say to their masters, Bring and let us drink. The Lord God hath sworn by His holiness that lo, the day shall come upon you that He will take away...take you away with hooks and your posterity with fish hooks and you shall go out at the breeches every cow at that which is before her and you shall cast them into the palace, saith the Lord.*" A time of devastating destruction.

In the eighth chapter of Amos and verse 4, and this is very powerful, "*Hear this, O you that swallow up the needy, even to make the poor of the land to fall, or fail, saying, When will the new moon be gone that we may sell grain?*" In other words, let's get this religious holiday over so we can get back to business, we're losing money. "*And the sabbath that we may set forth wheat making the ephah small and the shekel great and falsifying the balances by deceit?*" In other words, putting less in an ephah which is a measure of weight than supposedly was to be there and charging them more, paying more but getting less, falsifying the balances, deceit. They hated the feasts because it ground business to a halt.

"*Saying that we may buy the poor for silver and the needy for a pair of shoes, yea and sell the refuse of the wheat. The Lord has sworn by the excellency of Jacob, surely I will never forget any of your works. Shall not the land tremble for this and everyone mourn that dwells in it? And it shall rise up wholly like the river and be cast out and drown as by the river of Egypt. It will come to pass in that day, says the Lord God, that I will cause the sun to go down at noon, I will darken the earth in the clear day, I will turn your feasts into mourning and all your songs into lamentation. I will bring up sackcloth upon all loins and baldness on every head. I will make it like mourning for an only son and the end of it like a bitter day.*" This is just the prophetic denunciation against the wicked wealthy, and this is where James gets his heritage in terms of how he handles them in his epistle.

Now just to note so that you'll identify the direction of his text here, he is speaking and writing to the congregation of the church, those who are assembled in the name of Christ.

Some of them, obviously, claiming to be Christians weren't and that's why you have this series of tests, just as you do in 1 John. Some of them by their use of and abuse of wealth and money and material things showed utter disregard for God, utter disregard for His Word and demonstrated that in spite of their claim they did not possess salvation.

And I don't believe there's any way to equivocate on who he's speaking to here. Some have wanted to say he's not talking to people in the church, then why would he talk to them in the second person and why would he be speaking to people who aren't there to hear or reading to people who aren't there to listen?

The fact that he addresses them in the second person means that he has those in mind who will hear the letter, who had attached themselves to the church in some way. It would be pointless for him to be giving this kind of message to outsiders. Maybe if it was in the third person and he said, "You tell them what I want them to know," but this direct approach assumes their presence and that they would be in the sound of the hearing of this letter when it was read to the whole church.

These are people who, to some degree or other, want to be identified with God, to some degree or other want to have Christ in their life. But they don't come on God's terms.

Jesus also faced the reality that this would be the case. Do you remember in the parable of the soils in Matthew

13 how He talked about a certain kind of soil that was rocky? On the top it was soft and fertile but down a little ways into it, just below where the plow pulled its way through the dirt there was rock bed. And He said when the seed goes into there its roots go down and they begin to flourish and the plant comes up, but pretty soon the roots can't penetrate, they hit rock, they can't go down to get water.

When the sun comes out it burns the plant and it dies. Jesus describes those kinds of people as those who hear the Word, receive it with joy for a little while but when there's a price to pay, when they have to give up something, when they have to suffer for Christ, they don't want that, they leave.

Then He talked about a weedy soil, where the ground is still full of the roots of weeds. And though the good plant appears to come up, the weeds choke it out. And this is what He says of that in verse 32, "He that receives seed among the weeds is the one who hears the Word and the care of this age...listen to this...and the deceitfulness of riches chokes the Word and he becomes unfruitful."

There are people who hear the Word, they want to identify with the church, they may want what salvation promises but they're too deceived by riches and too in love with the world and too unwilling to sacrifice to let go. And while they may outwardly name the name of Christ, if their heart is not toward God and their heart is not toward heaven as indicated by where their treasure is, then no matter what their claim, they don't know the Lord.

It's like that parable of the pearl of great price and the treasure in a field, in both cases the man who wanted to buy the treasure and the man who wanted to buy the pearl sold all that he had to buy it. These are people who don't want to give up anything. They want their materialism, their wealth, their wickedness and Jesus on top. And in Matthew 19, Jesus wouldn't tolerate that with the rich young ruler. He said, "Sell everything you have, give the money to the poor and come and follow Me." And the man was very sad and went away. He loved his riches more than Christ.

I would venture to say that it's a sad thing but today we have given a lot of people the illusion that they're Christians because they talk a lot about Jesus but if you look at their life style, you're going to see that they betray that their real God is money and wealth. And may I go so far as to say some of them may be *TV evangelists*. And if you get behind the scenes of all the Jesus talk and start to see where they put their treasure, you're going to find out where their heart is.

They love money. These people love possessions. Their treasure is on the earth. And that's where their heart is. And they serve money. And so they can't serve God.

Back to James 4:4, "*Don't you know that friendship with the world is enmity with God? And whosoever therefore would be the friend of the world is the enemy of God.*" If you're into everything the world has to offer, you show your colors. John said, "*Love not the world, neither the things that are in the world. If any man love the world, the love of the Father is not in him,*" 1 John 2:15.

So the denunciation is directed at the rich fakers in the church who want to name the name of Jesus but whose real God is money. We can't allow people to live under the illusion that they're Christians and that Jesus talk is sufficient when one look at their life shows they are absolutely consumed with the love of money.

Now at the same time you say, "Is this directed just to those people?" And I say no. It also speaks to my heart and it speaks to your heart too as Christians. Because it reminds us of the sins of the fakers that we ought to avoid. It reminds us that we don't want to be anything like these people who outwardly name the name of Christ.

It's a strong warning of judgment against the wicked wealthy who are identified with the church but whose hearts are toward their money and whose God is their money and whose life surrounds their own personal comfort and indulgence. But it's also a great statement to those who are true believers to be sure we avoid the sins that characterize these people.

Now let's begin with the pronouncement that comes in verse 1. And it is a strong announcement of judgment. "*Come now, you rich men, weep and howl for your miseries that shall come upon you.*" Now with that call for the wicked wealthy to respond appropriately, James begins his denunciation. He is saying inescapable doom is coming and you ought to have the reaction of weeping and howling. The words "*come now*" you'll note are also back in verse 13 of chapter 4. He uses that little phrase twice.

Here it introduces a new group, there it introduced the kind of people who just lived their life without a thought for God. Here it introduces the wicked wealthy. It could be translated "*now listen*," or "*get this*" or "*see here*." It's calling their attention. It's...it's an attack in an Old Testament prophetic style. He calls them to stick up their ears and listen. And so he says, "*Come now, you rich men*," and that's the group he's attacking. That's the group he's denouncing...the materially wealthy who are wickedly wealthy.

Now do you remember who are the wealthy of the world? Do you remember when we defined that in our study of 1 Timothy? And we said that anybody is rich who has more than he...what?...needs. If you have what you need, you have no discretion with your money; you have to use it all to survive. But if you have any discretionary money, you're in the category of the rich. So who are the wealthy? Those people who have more than they need to live.

But who are the wicked wealthy to whom James speaks? They are the ones who misuse and utterly abuse the stewardship of that discretionary money. And so he's directing his attention to those whose lives are a continual abuse of their resources.

Notice what he tells them to do. "Weep and howl," two very interesting words, "weep and howl," means to sob out loud, it's not a silent crying. It means to sob out loud. It means to weep in a lamenting way. In fact, it is used for the wailing for the dead.

You'll see it in the seventh chapter of Luke, verses 13 and 32, and pointedly you'll see it in John 11 in the wailing, weeping at the tomb of Lazarus. It was used for those sort of public wailings that went on at the time of a death. It is also used for the weeping and the wailing out loud that comes as a result of shame and regret. We see it so used in Luke 7:38 and Matthew 26:75. So it speaks of a verbal vocal loud lamenting wailing kind of sorrow, strong emotional outbursts as people see the inescapable damning judgment of hell facing them. That's the idea. Now that you can see what you're really looking at, you better cry out loud, weep and lament.

By the way, the same word is used back in chapter 4 verse 9 where it says, "Be afflicted, mourn and weep," there it is the sorrow of repentance but here there is no call for repentance. And so another word is added here.

With repentance there is a loud lamenting and John shared in his testimony that when he begins to think about his sin he cries out to God about that. There is a lament, I think, in the heart of anyone who faces God and confesses sin. But it ends at that point because where there is the lament of repentance there is the grace of forgiveness.

But where there is the lament here, there is no grace and so the lament goes to a howl. It goes beyond that, ololuzo, an almost onomatopoetic word in the Greek, it means to shriek or to scream or to howl out loud beyond just lamenting, screaming, shrieking, shrill voice. It intensifies the outburst of despair, violent uncontrollable grief.

There are examples of this particularly in the Old Testament. The grief and the crying out and the howling of those who realize that they have committed the worst imaginable, the worst conceivable sins. You find it in the prophets. And in the present tense here, both of these verbs are saying "keep on lamenting, keep on screeching, shrieking, howling over your impending damnation." Very, very strong words.

So James calls for a frantic response of overwhelming grief. Why? Look at verse 1 again. "Because, or for, your miseries that shall come upon you." That word "miseries" used only here and Romans 3:16 has to do with wretchedness. It has to do with trouble beyond trouble, overwhelming trouble, overwhelming suffering, and overwhelming distress.

And it's your miseries, he's personalizes it, the miseries that are coming specifically on you. It's not generic. He's not saying collectively all of you should howl because collectively you're all going to suffer, he's saying you individually ought to howl because you're individually going to suffer misery.

He doesn't tell us when it's coming but we know when it's coming, it's coming at the coming of Christ. It's coming when they meet God. Judgment is inevitable. That's the cry here...judgment on the wicked wealthy.

In Luke chapter 6 and verse 24, "*Woe unto you that are rich for you have received your consolation. Woe unto you that are full for you will hunger. Woe unto you that laugh now for you will mourn and weep.*" What statements, what fearful statements. I remember what Peter said to Simon in Acts 8, "*Your money perish with you.*" If you live for money, you die, you perish and may your money perish along with you.

So in the Old Testament, from the lips of our Lord and here from James, pronouncements of judgment on the wicked wealthy. But why? What is it that these people did that brings about this punishment?

Let's look at the first of the four characteristics of the wicked wealthy that result in their judgment and you just see how pertinent this first point is. They will be damned because, number one, their wealth was...get this...uselessly hoarded. Did you get that? Uselessly hoarded, verses 2 and 3. This is a damning thing. "*Your riches are corrupted, your garments are moth-eaten, your gold and silver are rusted and the rust of them shall be a witness against you and shall eat your flesh as it were fire, you have hoarded wealth for the last days, or in the last days...*better translation." The sin is mentioned at the end of verse 3, you have hoarded it, you have...the verb is the verb from which we get the word thesaurus; you have heaped up your hoarded treasure. You have stockpiled your wealth.

You say, "Is that wrong?" Yes because it's to the exclusion of its proper use. You have uselessly piled it up.

Boy, that's a tragic sin of our own time. Obviously when God prospers you and me and gives us more than we need, He does it that we might use it properly for His glory and to the advance of His Kingdom. My approach to life says that I want to go out of this world just at the time my money runs out.

I want to make sure that I'm not hoarding up against some nebulous tomorrow that may never come when God is calling for the proper investment of all that I have into His eternal Kingdom right now.

Obviously God provides for us so that we might provide for our families. And he that doesn't do that, 1 Timothy 5 says, is worse than an unbeliever. We are to take care of our family, of those in the extended family, of those bereft and widowed women who are known to us. Beyond that, every other part of the money that God has given us and the wealth He has given us is to be used somehow for His glory. Scripture tells us that some of it is to be devoted to His service.

In the Old Testament they gave it to the temple. They gave it even to the building of the tabernacle. They gave to God regularly what God desired from them, some tithes which they had to give and many, many freewill offerings which they gave out of the willingness of their heart. It is to be devoted to His service.

Jesus said, Luke 6:38, "*Give and it shall be given unto you, pressed down, shaken together and running over shall men give into your bosom.*" The Apostle Paul wrote and said, "The first day of the week let each one of you lay by him and store as God has prospered him." So our wealth is to be given to the kingdom. It is to be given to the expansion of the Kingdom, to the extension of the Kingdom.

Not as a legalistic enterprise but because our hearts are so consumed with the mission of the Kingdom and with the love of the Lord who is the King.

Thirdly, not only is it to be used on the family God has given us and devoted to the service of the Kingdom, but thirdly it is to be used to win the lost. I can't think of anything better to do with money than to invest it in those who win the lost. In Luke 16 in a very, very direct statement regarding the use of money Jesus said, "*Make to yourselves friends by means of the money of unrighteousness that when it fails they may receive you into everlasting habitation.*" In other words, use your money to make friends who will greet you in heaven when you get there. Use your money to win people to Christ, what else? Uselessly hoarding it violates God's intention.

Fourthly, the Scripture says use your money to care for the needy. I read you those passages in the Old Testament and every one of the prophetic diatribes against the wicked are basically because they defrauded the poor and the needy and the fatherless and the widow.

They held back from those in need and John says in 1 John 3 that if you close up your compassion to that kind of person then you tell me how the love of God dwells in you...if you hoard your money rather than give it to those in need. Even the Apostle Paul in Galatians 2 spoke so directly about how important it was to remember the poor and said, "I also was diligent to do that."

Providing for your family, devoting it to the service of the Kingdom, using it to win the lost, caring for those in need and then a fifth we could add, support people who minister. Galatians 6:6 says, "Let the one who is taught share in the one who teaches in all...share with the one who teaches in all good things." "The servant is worthy of his hire." "Feed the ox that treads out the grain." In other words, support the ministry.

You have been given wealth by God...use it for the care of the people God has given you. Use it to devote to His service. Use it to win the lost. Use it to care for those in need. Use it to support those in ministry. But don't hoard it.

And if it has been your characteristic to hoard it all uselessly, then says James you'll be damned for such and evidence of the fact that your heart is set on earthly things and your God is money, not the true God. There's no place for saying you're a believer, you're a true child of God, you're a lover of Christ, a servant of God and then amassing a fortune, uselessly stashed away without regard for God's Word at all.

James depicts this kind of hoarding. Look at the way he depicts it. He mentions, first of all, riches corrupted; secondly, garments moth-eaten; thirdly, gold and silver rusted. Now apart from land and houses, and we'll just cover this briefly so stay with me, apart from land and houses, wealth really was involved with those three things.

First, the riches generally refer to food...grain, wheat, barley, perhaps even some meat that would be stored that was susceptible to decay. The term "decay" I think gives us the latitude to translate the word "riches" or at least to see that it has the sense of food, that which can easily decay.

People put their wealth in stockpiling grain, like the rich fool whose barns were full. He said pull them down, build greater barns, store it all there. Eat, drink and be merry, in other words, I'll live out my life, I'll never work again, I've got it all stashed forever. And that is the evidence of an unregenerate heart, laziness. I've got it all piled up. And of course that was typical in that day, stock up your grain and live off it the rest of your life, amass as much as you can for yourself...uselessly hoarding it. And they did that with grain, stockpiling it.

The word "riches," by the way, is the word ploutos. And the word comes from the name of one of the ancient Greek gods of mythology. His name Ploutos means the abundant yielding of the earth. So that's really what that word means. And by the way, he was said in Greek mythology to be the son of Demetra, the goddess of the earth. So the word ploutos then has a connection through Greek mythology with what the earth produces and thereby we also can conclude that it can be used to refer to the food, vegetables, grain and perhaps even meat that are stored up as a result of the products of the earth.

But James says they are rotted, they are corrupted. The noun form of that verb is used for a putrefying sore and speaks of corrupting decay. It's sort of like the manna in the Old Testament, if you gathered for two days what you gathered over what you needed corrupted. So he says all your hoarded grain is rotted. And the picture here is not of a judgment but of a reality. You can't keep it, it will rot. You can't stockpile it, it will decay. Your hoarding is so useless because in the end it's going to be no good to anybody.

Then secondly, rich people put their money and their fortune into garments. And he uses the word garment here, himatia, it means the loose long outer robe, they would put rich embroidery and jewelry. Those robes were passed on as heirlooms. And you could literally have a fortune in your garments.

Of course, when those garments were folded and stacked somewhere as you well know, the larva of moth could ruin them...ruin them. And garments as our Lord even talked about could be moth eaten. And so if you're stockpiling your treasure in grain and that, it's going to get rotted given enough time. If you stockpile it in garments, they're going to be moth-eaten given enough time.

And then thirdly, your gold and silver have rusted, corroded. Obviously the coinage of that day of which James refers is like the coinage of which our Lord referred in Matthew 6 where He said, "*Lay up your treasure in heaven where moth and rust do not corrupt.*"

The implication is, and we have some research to back it up, that coins in those days were not pure silver or pure gold but mixed with an alloy tended given the right circumstances to rust indeed. And James says money stashed somewhere over the long period of time, buried in the ground, may itself rust. And then what do you have...then what do you have? Nothing.

James' point is so basic. How sinful, how foolish, how stupid to hoard money, to hoard clothing, to hoard food when it all rots. And even if it remains, you won't. And if that's the way you've lived your life, the question is whether you worship God at all.

We hoard so many things. Stocks, bonds, savings account, gold, silver, jewelry, possessions. Where is your treasure? Where is it invested? Where are you piling it up? We hoard so many things.

I don't want you to be irresponsible about your life. But I want you to know that you can't hoard it. Somebody said, "If money talks, all it ever says to me is goodbye." And there's no question about that. So before it can say goodbye, why don't you use it for the glory of God?

Well, from there he talks about the judgment on them. Just quickly, verse 3, "The rust itself," and now he's sort of personalizes the rust, he makes it come alive, "*And the rust is a witness against you when you face God, your rust will rise up and testify to your ungodliness.*" It will testify to your hoarding. It will testify to your stockpiling.

And the ruin of the things the rich hoarded is a graphic picture of their own ruin. Their hoarded rotted moth-eaten rusted riches give loud testimony to the state of their heart. The rotting corroded riches that are hoarded become the witness at the divine court to bring unarguable evidence for their eternal damnation, their covetous selfish compassionless earthbound approach to life becomes in itself their condemnation.

All that hoarded wealth is witness for the prosecution declaring their guilt and the just God to condemn them to hell.

And then the rust is personalized not only to be a witness but the rust becomes the executioner. And he says it will eat your flesh as it were fire. And he personalizes the rust into fire and the rust which first of all was the decaying element, the personalized becomes the witness and then personalized becomes the executioner. Rust moves slow but this rust acts like fire and fire is the fastest consumer of all. Corrosion may be slow but fire is the fastest destroyer.

In the Day of Judgment the rust of your hoarded goods will rise up to testify against you and become the fire that burns you fleshes...plural. Very interesting that James uses the plural because he's not talking about a group he's talking about individuals again. Each one of your flesh will burn as your own riches rise up to be your executioner.

By the way, that's a reminder that hell is a physical place. Your fleshes will burn there. That is a physical place. There is real burning there. There is a fire that is not quenched and you will have, according to John 5, a resurrected body suited to bear the punishment of an eternal hell and feel the flame forever and never be consumed. That hell is reserved for people who hoarded their treasure. Hell is for hoarders of treasure.

And he closes by saying you have hoarded wealth, no Kingdom investment, uselessly stockpiling your goods, rotting away without regard for God, for Christ, for others and you're headed for hell and that will be a witness against you. And then he adds this final note. "*And you've done it in these last days*," the Greek text says. You've done it in these last days. In other words, you lived without regard for redemptive history. You did it in the Messianic period.

These last days are from the first coming of Christ to His Second Coming. John says, "My little children, it is the last time," 1 John chapter 2 verse 17. We're in the last days. Christ has appeared once in the end of the age.

This is the last time. And so what you've done is hoarded your wealth in the last days with no regard for God's clock, no regard for redemptive history, no regard for eternity, totally wasted your life and all your resources. How bizarre. How utterly unthinkable, amassing wealth in a day when the world is perishing.

If people who represent Jesus Christ really were concerned about lost people going to hell and really were concerned about reaching the world for Jesus Christ, they would not be buying half a dozen homes, having millions of dollars in bank accounts, spending millions of dollars on cars and other personal items and spending a fortune to pad their own seat.

That's a dead giveaway as to where somebody's heart is. I don't care who they say they represent. There is a betrayal of what's really in the heart.

There is no way you can affirm the salvation of a person like that. Now God knows, I don't know that, but I certainly stand and say they don't seem to pass the test.

They who in the name of Jesus Christ claim to want to reach a world but busy themselves amassing a fortune illegitimately for themselves. That's absolutely inconsistent with any commitment to be consumed to win a lost world to the Savior.

To have the heart of Jesus is to reach out with what you have to people who don't have what they need, not to consume things on your own lust.

The only acceptable way to live in the light of the Second Coming of Christ in these last days of redemptive history is to live holding very loosely the wealth that God gives you and to make sure you're using it for His glory.

If you've been living an illusion about your Christianity but when you self-examine a little bit you see your real God is money, then bow the knee to Jesus before it's too late.

If as a Christian you find yourself infringing in this area of sin, ask God's Spirit to root it out of your life, loosen your grip on the things of this world and give you the heart of the prophet who sees all things to be used for the glory of God and anything hoarded is rotted.

God gives us new things every day. He wouldn't let them take manna for more than one day. The ground replenishes our food every season.

We don't need to hoard against the unknown future. We need to invest in the eternal Kingdom with the promise that God will never allow His people to want if they're faithful to Him.

And so the point I want you to see here is that James is saying you start out amassing. Your amassed fortune in part is due to defrauding others. You then begin to spend it on your lusts which are so consumed that you literally destroy people in the process...you destroy them.

And why the condemnation of the rich? Because of their useless hoarding, their unjust robbery, their self-indulgent spending and their ruthless acquisition. Fulfilling their lusts at the expense of the destruction of anybody and everybody who gets in their way.

What a...what a travesty, what a frightening way to waste the substance that God has given us.

11. CONCLUSION

It is better to gather ones riches in heaven than on earth. The devil only uses money as another way of getting control over our lives, so that we ultimately lose our salvation.

As I have illustrated in this book, it is very easy for a rich person to become corrupted by money and very difficult to turn back.

Rich people totally concerned with luxury and pleasure can't restrain themselves. A man with money closes his eyes to the needs of other people, closes his eyes to the work of God, but has his wide open to his own self-gratification.

The rich lives to gratify himself. I watch these people spend money like drunken sailors. It's absolutely beyond comprehension. And then to indulge themselves in every imaginable vice...

Now you know why it is easier for a Camel to go through a needle's eye, than for a rich man to enter into the Kingdom of God…

www.ingramcontent.com/pod-product-compliance
Ingram Content Group UK Ltd.
Pitfield, Milton Keynes, MK11 3LW, UK
UKHW041902190726
13854UKWH00003B/1034

9 781300 429692